FOUNDATION IN FASHION DESIGN AND ILLUSTRATION

JULIAN SEAMAN

D0317899

B T BATSFORD
LONDON

Text and illustrations © Julian Seaman 2001
The moral right of the author has been asserted

ISBN 0 7134 8703 8

Designed by Wladek Szechter

Printed and bound in Spain

First published in 2001
by B.T. Batsford Ltd
9 Blenheim Court
Brewery Road
London N7 9NY

A member of the Chrysalis Group plc

Contents

Introduction

Aspiring designers have often decided to focus on fashion design, long before they apply to art school. Although not the only avenue to professional fulfilment, art schools remain the springboard for the majority of visually creative people.

In the world of fashion, however, it is important for potential students to be sure in themselves whether they fall into the area of keen fashion consumer, follower and – in some cases – victim, or actual creative instigator and designer. Many potential fashion students look the part, act the part but then fall apart when confronted with the reality: hard work and talent will always triumph over pose and attitude.

Having said that, no-one should forget the essential frivolity and fun of an ephemeral art form. Fashion has a large part to play in popular culture – both reflecting and projecting the zeitgeist – and it is an enormous international business. However, a lightness of touch and natural ability help no end. It is only frock and toile, but we like it!

A general art training and awareness is essential to any designer. Working in a vacuum without influences is seldom productive and, although many potential fashion designers may have already chosen their specialist area during school, exposure to fine art, film, graphics, product design and any number of areas can only make them better designers in their chosen sphere. Even though, in many professions, specialisation and streamlining now happen earlier and earlier, the broader picture must never be forgotten. Many hopeful fashion students fall into various traps, which this book should help them avoid – not least of which is trying too hard. I have seen many pre-art school portfolios that have painstakingly depicted 'fashion design drawings', and on every page a completely different combination of shapes and colours is presented. This represents an enormous amount of wasted effort; each of those drawings could have spawned a hundred variations. There is no need to 're-invent the wheel' with every picture.

There is a big difference between trying too hard and working very hard. This book should help separate the two by encouraging the latter and describing the pitfalls of the former.

In no way would I claim that this is the only way to achieve results. Students will always benefit from a mixture of different tutors and influences, but the logical progression of this book should blow away any preconceived ideas, instil confidence in any fashion student and let them progress into their own creative mould.

Paper Collage

Drawing is an essential skill for designers to master if they are to express their ideas on paper; however, it is the ideas that are the most important.

The drawing abilities of students vary so much and at the very beginning I don't like to discourage the weaker draftsman who may have great ideas. I start with images created by collage that uses only tone.

Newsprint text comes in many densities, and the areas of grey to black vary so much that this exercise encourages the search for tonal values and a general illustrative awareness, without the need for drawing skills.

It is often useful to start by basing the illustration on an existing image so that you can test your skills at tone matching.

This may not seem particularly relevant to fashion, but it provides a good introduction to image and technique.

Most of this book's project ideas involve a specific task with an underlying lesson that is learnt at the same time.

In this case, a great image can be achieved without drawing, and at the same time the observational properties of tone are explored.

A 'found' picture is a good starting point, and in fashion terms any past icon could work well.

9 PAPER COLLAGE

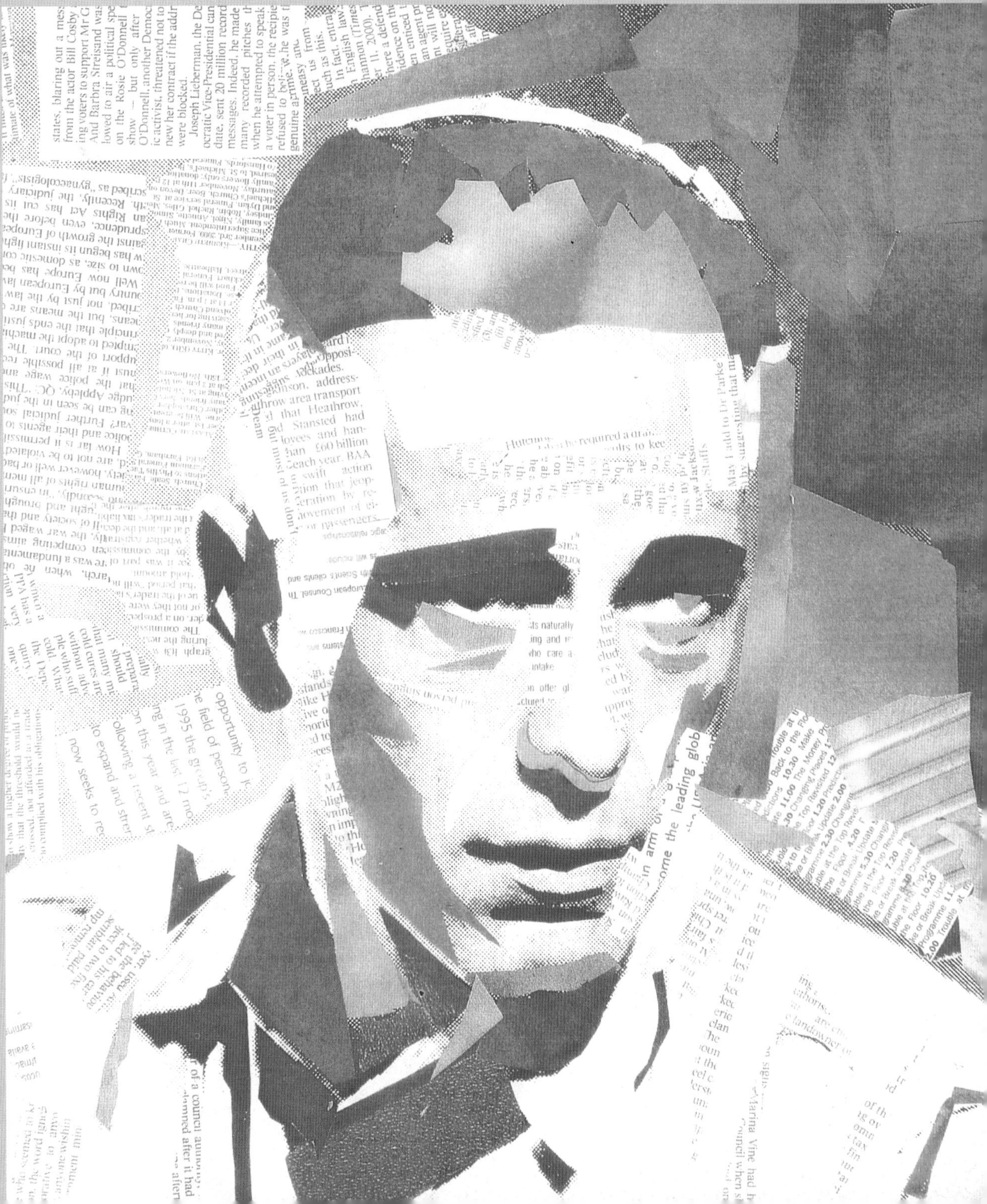

Having used recognisable images, it can be fun to
experiment with your own creations and try
different colour-ways with them.

Using a photocopier as a tool can be productive. Flat reproduction gives a new dimension to your collage. You can take this a stage further by colour photocopying one image on acetate and re-copying it with a paper print to achieve a 'doubling' effect.

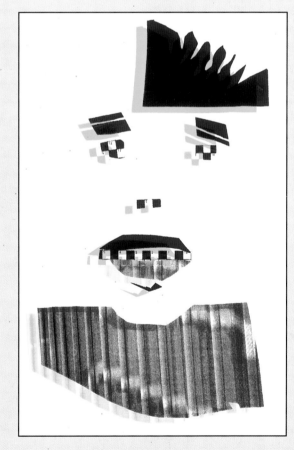

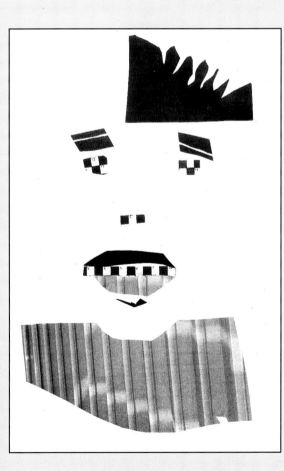

At the end of this short project you will certainly
have some interesting graphic illustrations,
which will have been achieved without
drawing.

Creative Collage

Now it is time to let your imagination run wild.

Start by finding a
hoard of magazines
(by no means just
fashion), then go
through and cut out a
selection of heads.
Keep them in a pile, then go
through again and search for shapes –
bottles, watches, shoes, cars etc.

Now create figures using your 'found' material.

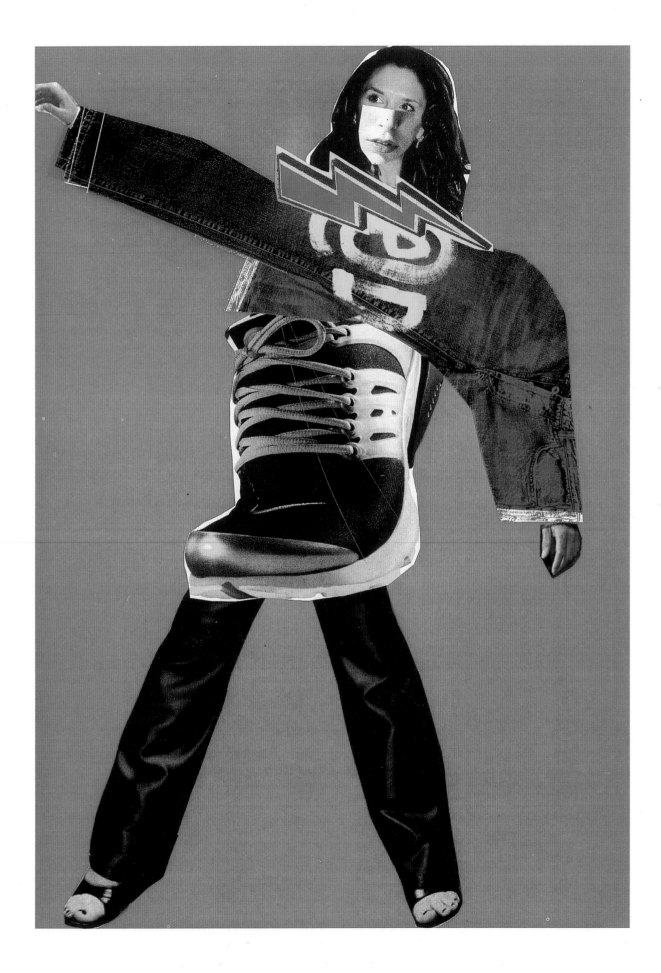

Your lateral thinking can take over, but soon
you will realise that, somewhere in
there, fashion ideas are emerging.
This, again, is where an appreciation of fine
art can spawn clothing inspiration.

It can become instant design, again without either drawing or making.

The creative channels are open, unencumbered.

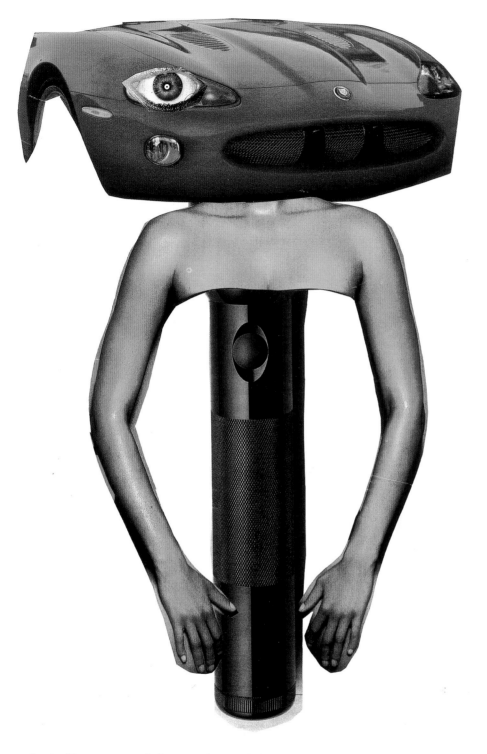

Some, if not many, of these early possibilities will be unworkable. No problem. At least a free idea has emerged.

Fashion designs change from season to season, but the method of designing them does not change very much.

This exercise is designed to release you from the worries of being able to draw, or even mix your colours.

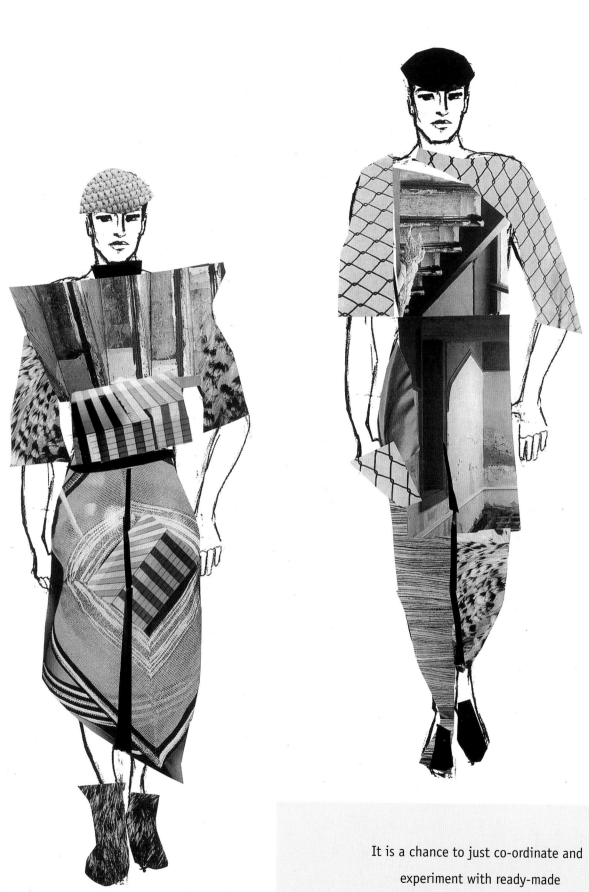

It is a chance to just co-ordinate and
experiment with ready-made
shapes, textures and colours.

This still isn't fashion design, but it is a stepping
stone on the way, without having to worry
about unintended colours and dodgy figures.
It also educates the eye to 'found' material
that has design potential.

Life Drawing

Although we have, so far, let you off as far as drawing is concerned, the importance of these skills must not be overlooked.

Life-drawing classes are essential, and a confident pencil line must be developed.

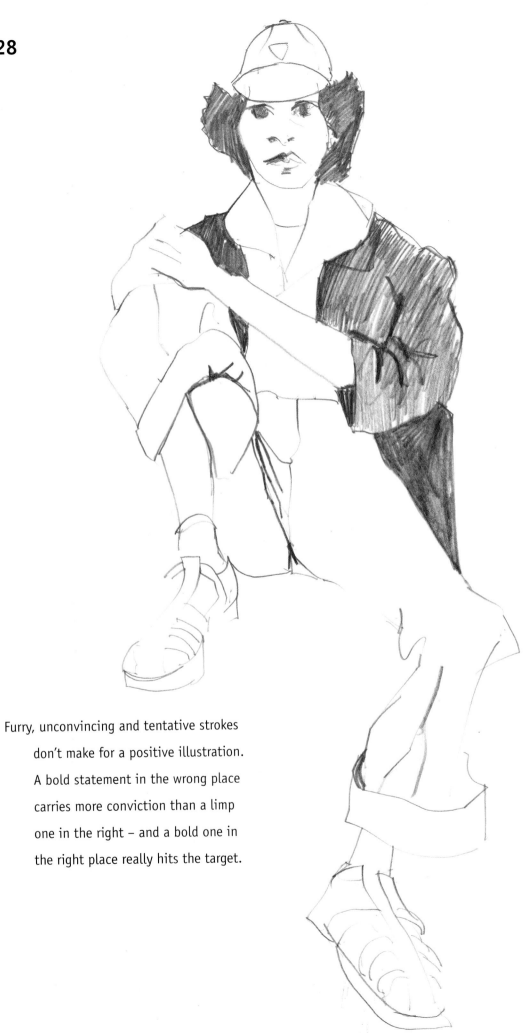

Furry, unconvincing and tentative strokes
don't make for a positive illustration.
A bold statement in the wrong place
carries more conviction than a limp
one in the right – and a bold one in
the right place really hits the target.

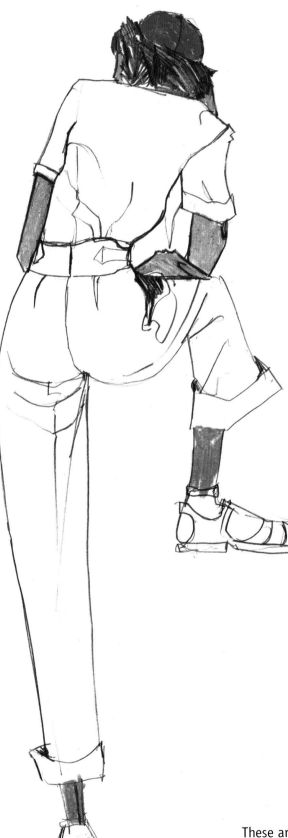

These are some examples of strong and confident pencil work from a couple of classes, with some bold but minimal added colour.

Always try to avoid being too literal.
With these two drawings, I
deliberately left out the means of
support (i.e. the steps or the seat)
to draw attention to the figures.

Try to keep well away from tightly
representational drawings. Use
big brushes, soft pencils and a
free hand.

Loosen Up

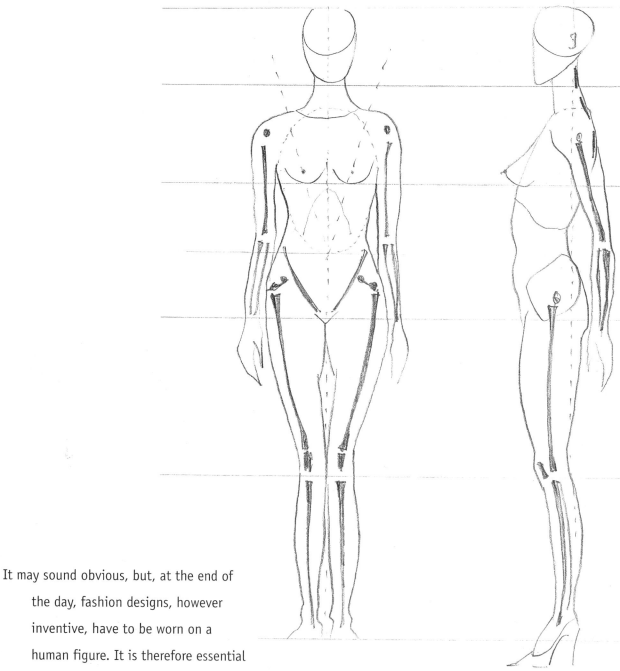

It may sound obvious, but, at the end of the day, fashion designs, however inventive, have to be worn on a human figure. It is therefore essential that human proportions are understood. Even though, in fashion drawing convention, the legs are elongated, the relative body masses and pivots remain constant.

Using these proportions, just doodle away at body shapes in all
sorts of free styles. Release yourself from the strictures of
tight linear representation and loosen up in shape, form,
colour and line.

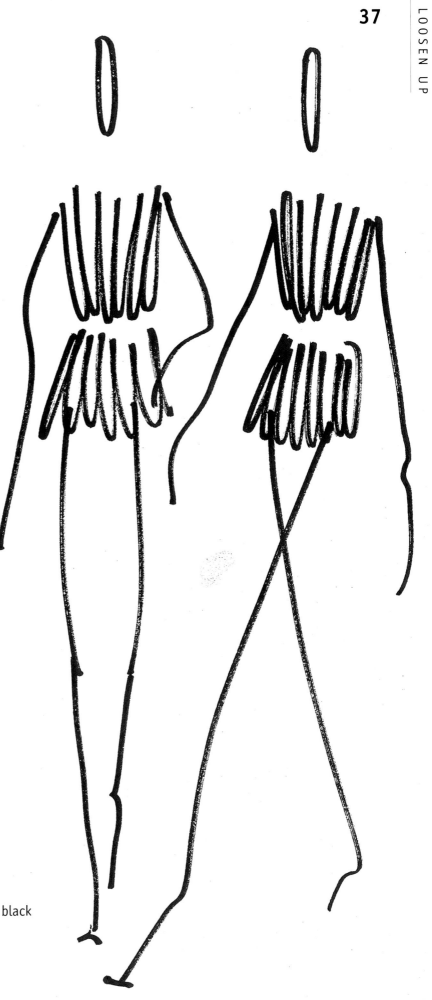

Try drawing figures in motion, using just a black
felt-tipped pen.

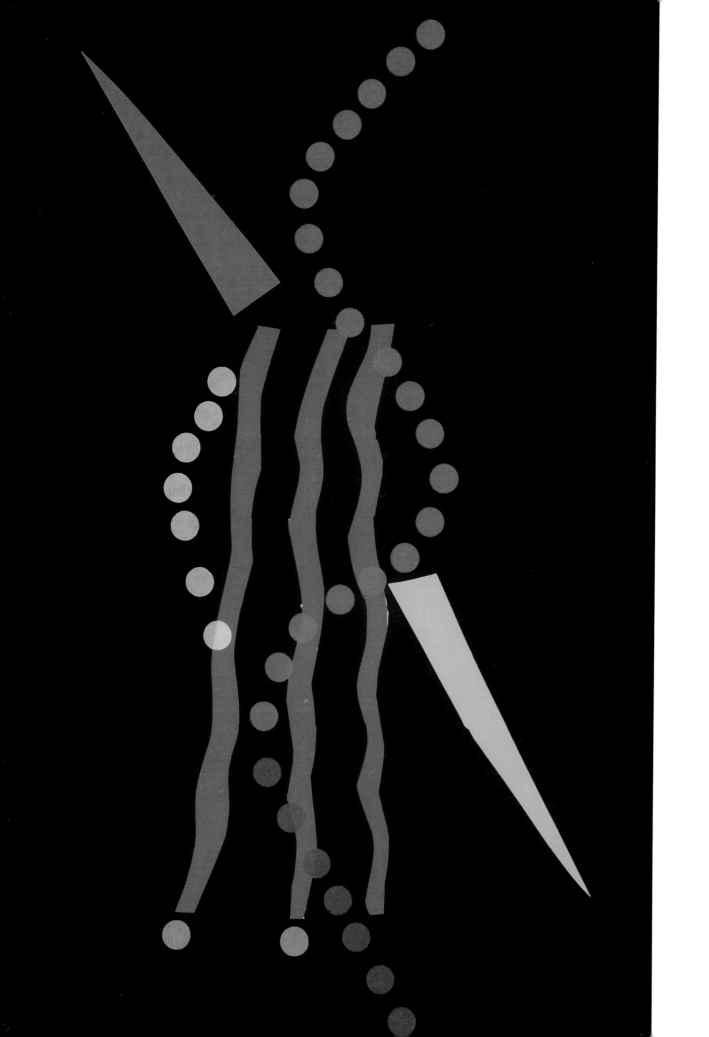

Be as bold and carefree as you can. If your first
 couple of efforts don't work, just have
 another go.

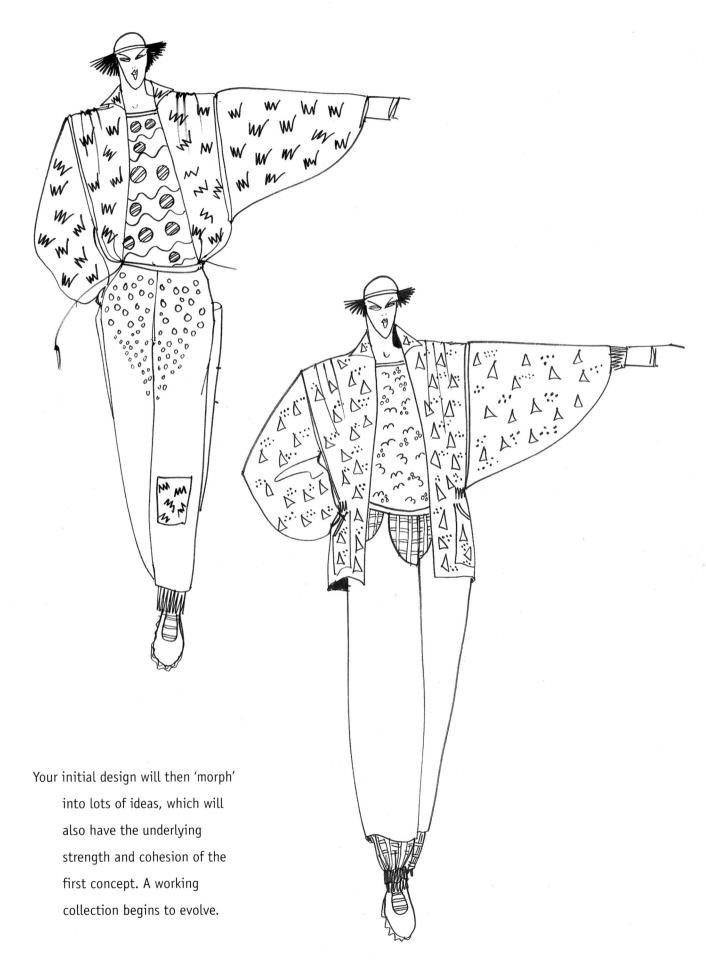

Your initial design will then 'morph' into lots of ideas, which will also have the underlying strength and cohesion of the first concept. A working collection begins to evolve.

Obviously, some ideas will work better than
others, but by this stage you should be able
to make your own value judgements.

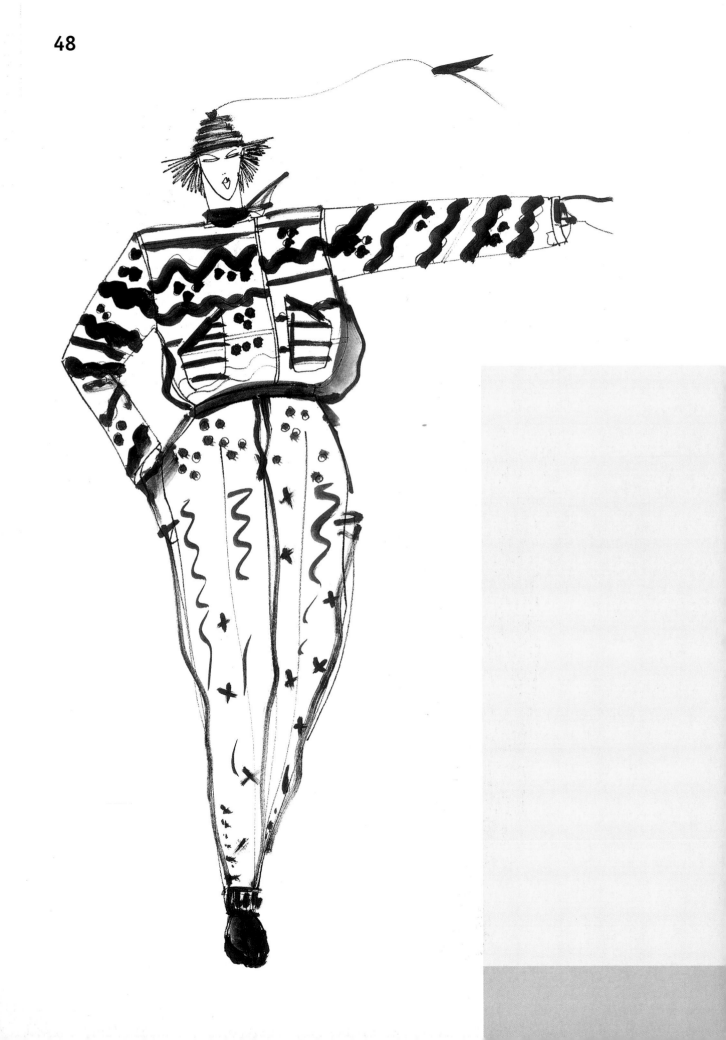

The next step is to choose around five of the twenty ideas and photocopy each one about four times.

By now your one source has multiplied, and your best ideas can be hit with different colour-ways.

This process is very liberating, since there is no
preciousness about finished drawings. Your working
area is only a photocopy of your own design, so
there is no need to draw and no need to worry that
one wrong move with a brush or pen might spoil
several hours' work. It is a chance to be bold,
because mistakes don't matter.

This system also provides a body of work, from which the
best ideas can be picked and then further developed.

This is a chance to try new colour-ways, textures, combinations and treats. It is always fun to allow yourself an indulgent design extravagance, whether it works or not. What's more, by using this method you can try all sorts and select the best.

Here is just a sample of possibilities:

Multiples

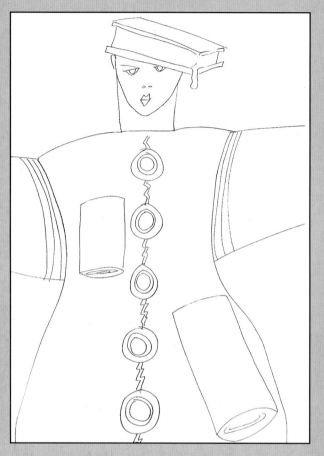

Another way of ensuring cohesion of
design in a collection or project
is a device I call 'factory drawing'.
The best analogy is to compare the
process to the print run of a book.
Again, the idea is to follow a simple
process from start to finish.
The added bonus is the skill learnt in
matching colour over a range
of illustrations; the process
guarantees this.
Firstly, you need four sheets of paper
to work on at the same time.
Draw a very simple design in four
variations, leaving spaces that can
be filled with colour.
This can be useful for potential
dress print designers, as the
question of how to cover certain
areas is more important than
cutting and sewing details.
Choose a palette of between four and six
colours, and reject all of your other
materials. These could be three
gouache paints and three oil
pastels, or any other combination.
Then, make a decision about the colour
balance of all four of your drawings.

Apply the first colour to all four pictures.

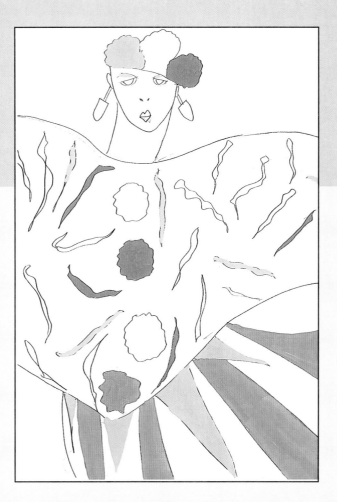

Then, methodically apply each
next colour in rotation.

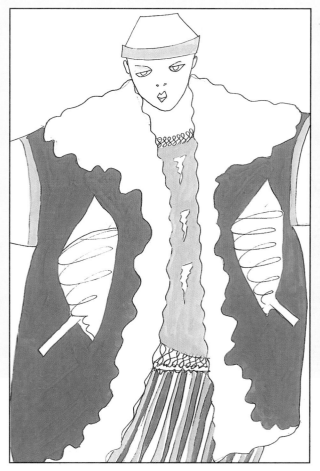

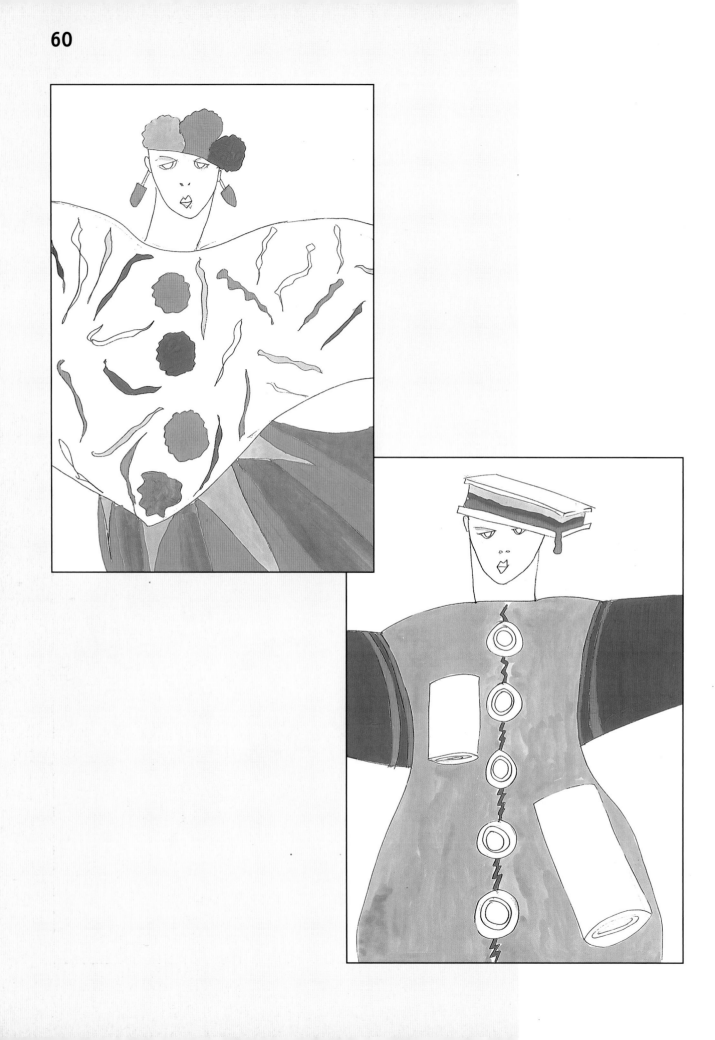

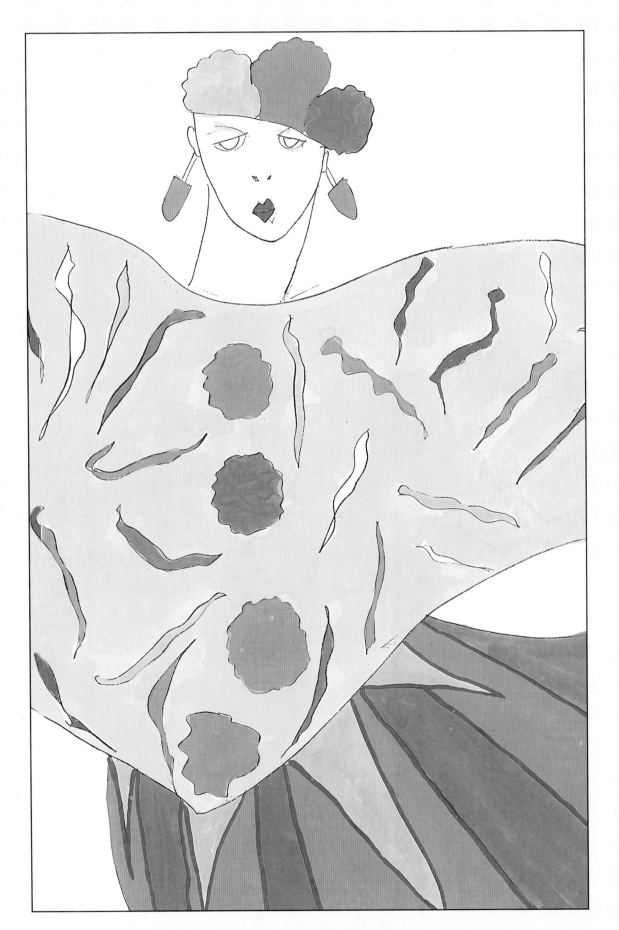

Here, the designs were inspired by pastel, 'ice-cream' colours and this led to the addition of details such as cones, cornets, wafers, Arctic Rolls, 99s and Neapolitans.

The final stage is to finish the faces and details.

The finished effect is a
comprehensive loc
to the collection.

Fine Art

Now, armed with drawing and painting skills (albeit at early stages), your
confidence should be increasing.

It is time to find other areas of inspiration, and examples from fine art can
be a great starting point, whether for colour ideas, structure, theme,
garment or print.

These following examples have been taken from a single painting by
Matisse.

Firstly, identify different areas of the painting to develop into print designs
that could work well together.

By painting and colour matching, combined with close observation of the original picture, you end up with fashion print ideas that still have the feel of the original picture. These can be expanded or reduced in scale.

To make these print ideas work on garment designs, you can return to the previous techniques.

Use a basic shape with which you have already worked. Photocopy it several times. Then, photocopy your print ideas in different scales and experimentally collage them onto your designs.

As ever, these ideas can trigger a further stage of development.

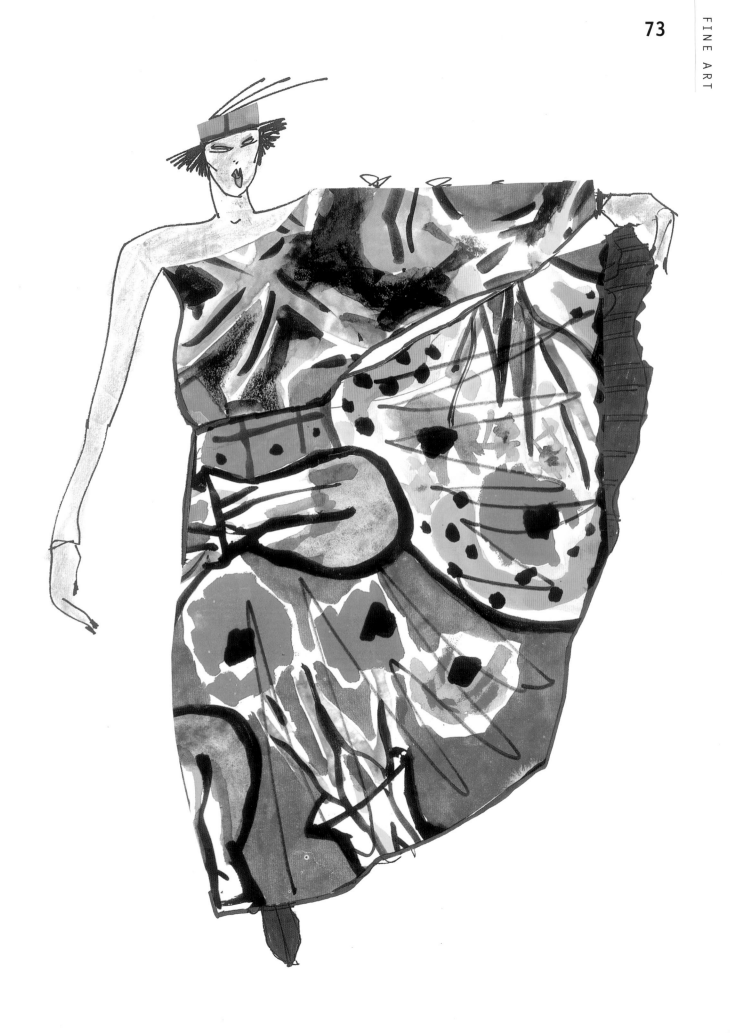

Inspiration from Swatches

Another line of inspiration for fashion designers is to source fabric samples and work on the combinations of different patterns.

Once again, this project is just a 'starter' to open up the potential of the next stage.

Here, I have found some samples and worked them together in various scales. This practice could be continued indefinitely.

You will notice that I have used another new style of illustration. Too many fashion students feel they need to invent their own stylised illustration technique. This can enormously restrict creative experiment; variety is much more important.

This exercise is meant to whet the
creative appetite.
By playing about with the textile
images, design ideas can emerge.

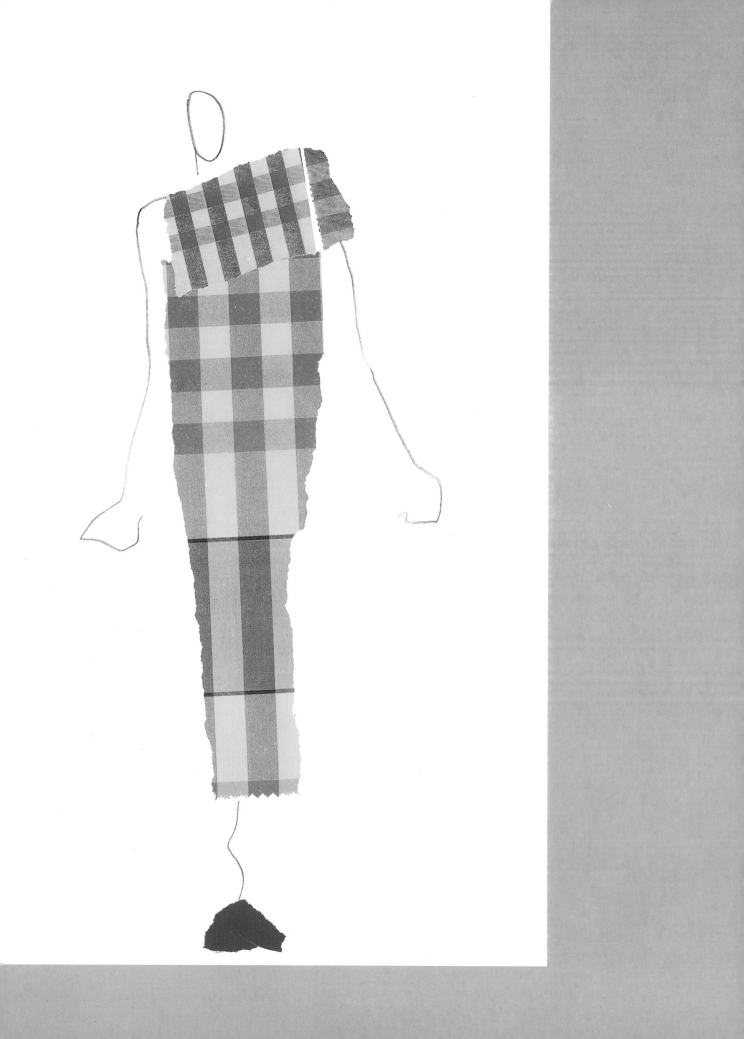

Concept Project

A different approach is to set yourself or to be set a project that requires an
in-depth look at the subject matter, through research, development of a
set brief and then concluding designs.

Here, the sample brief is a visit to the Victoria and Albert Museum, London to
observe the corsets, crinolines and bustles that shaped the silhouettes
of a generation. How could we use this inspiration to create a collection
that reflects the historical derivation, but creates
modern designs?

CURVACEOUS

BONED,BUSTY,BELLSHAPED AND BUSTLED

C.S.M. B.A. PROJECT WITH THE V&A 30 Oct 00 >Oct 01

The body silhouette continually changes with the dictates of fashion. Historically
designers have employed all kinds of undergarment structure to create the look. The
Victorian use of corsets, crinolines, bustles and bone achieved a voluptuous and
curvaceous outline which most recently has inspired designers such as Westwood
and McQueen.

At your visit to the V&A on Oct 30 you will see the collection of corsets,bustles etc.
and be talked through them by their curator Lucy Pratt.

Your brief is to design a garment inspired by what you have seen at the session.
Perhaps the curves above the structures give you ideas,or maybe the frames and
padding themselves.Whatever the inspiration,the design drawings will illustrate the
development of your ideas and show how the past can influence the future.

All designs and research will be judged on Fri 24 Nov and the top six will then start
to be made up. There is then a break until April 2001 when the final judging will take
place at a gala fashion show on April 23 at the V&A,to launch the Curvaceous
exhibition,which will include historical garments and the CSM finalists.These will be
on display until Oct 2001.

Curvaceous will be the first exhibition in the newly revamped Dress Gallery 40,one of
the most popular at the V&A.

Julian Seaman

bustle

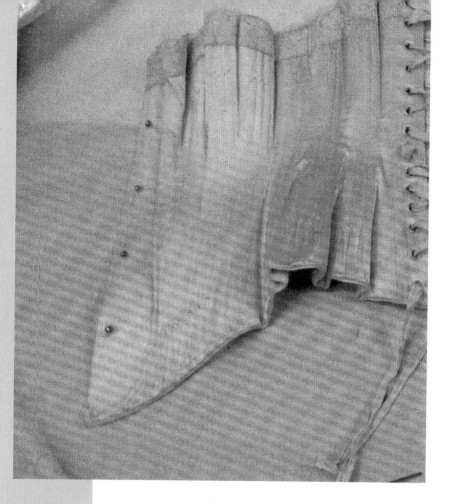

The first stage is to see the source material, take photographs and make notes of the details.

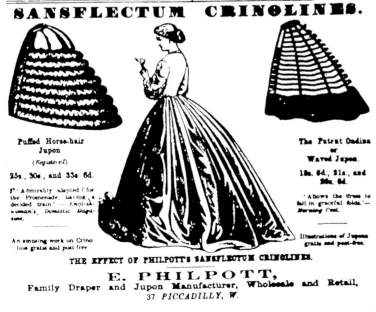

Next, find printed source material and start working into it. The ideas can be as experimental as you like.

It is impossible to reproduce, in a book, the whole sketch book approach, but I can show some examples of how a brief can be researched, how the research can lead to design ideas, then lead to a new approach and finally be illustrated as design concepts.

Your research book can include
attempts at some detailing. Here,
the lacing is explored.

Now it is time to start on some rough,
   almost doodled design ideas,
   inspired by your previous pages
   and working up your shapes and
   colour palette.

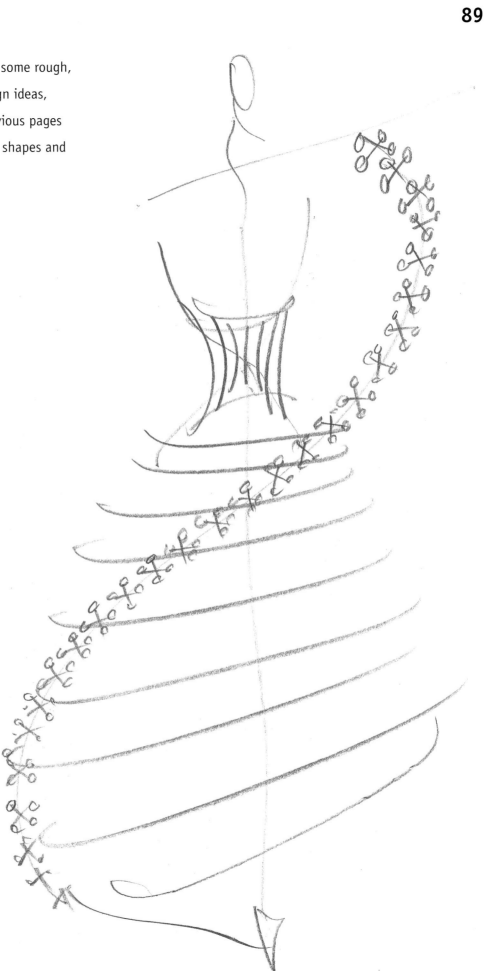

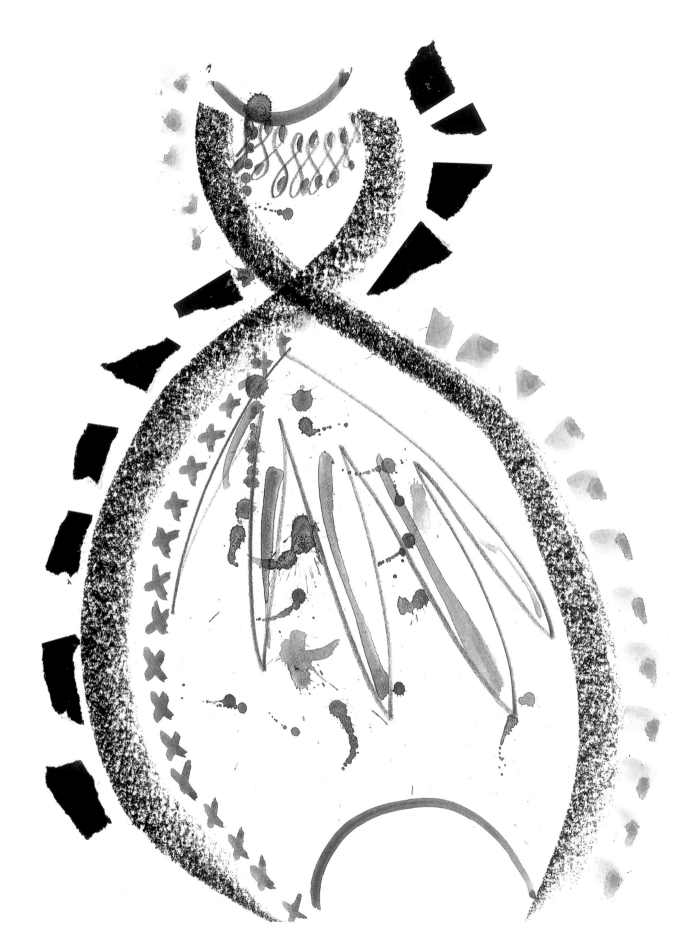

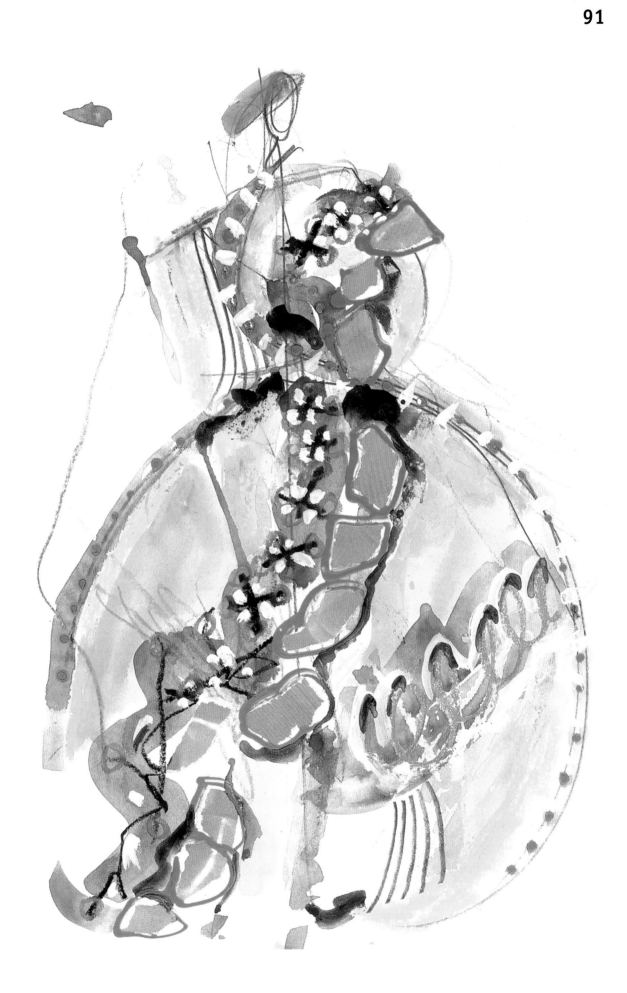

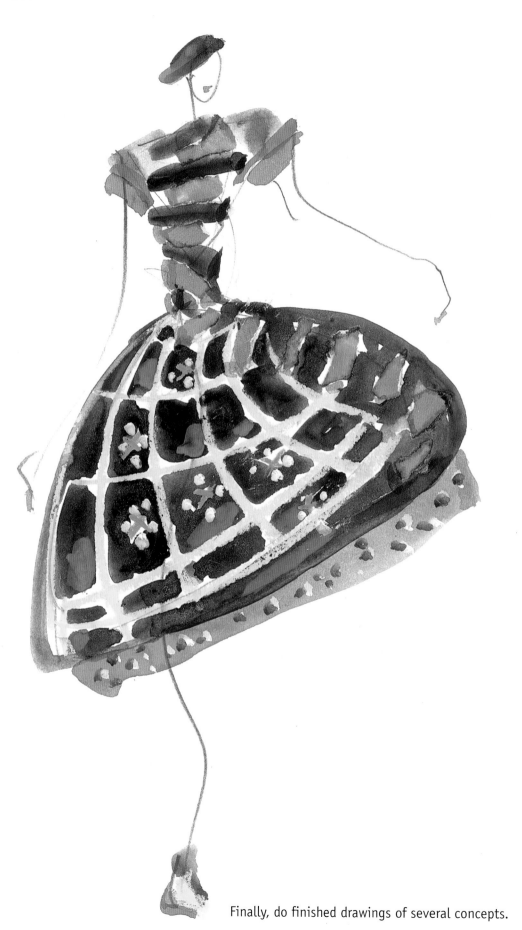

Finally, do finished drawings of several concepts.

Normally, this research and work would be presented in a sketch book bulging with inspiration and ideas, working through found objects, colour ideas, developments and then putting ideas to the body, design and final outcome. The fine art influences can be applied using a 'loosened-up' technique.

Conclusion

Ideas are the most important aspect of any artistic endeavour. However,
   you need certain skills in order to articulate these ideas.
This book is designed to strip away the mystique of how to find inspiration.
   There are many sources for this inspiration; these are only touched
   upon here, but the book should at least open your mind, ready to
   absorb and utilize aspects of everything that helps with your creation.
The drawings here are just one person's answer to his own questions, but
   hopefully they will point the way for you to find your own ideas.
Nothing is more exciting, for a tutor who also works in the design world,
   than to encourage a new talent to emerge.
Designing should be fun. I hope this book makes it easier for you to get
   onto the first rung of the ladder.